Easy Brown Rice Cookbook

50 Unique and Easy Brown Rice Recipes

By
BookSumo Press

Published by
http://www.booksumo.com

ENJOY THE RECIPES?

KEEP ON COOKING
WITH 6 MORE FREE COOKBOOKS!

Visit our website and simply enter your email address to join the club and receive your 6 cookbooks.

http://booksumo.com/magnet

https://www.instagram.com/booksumopress/

https://www.facebook.com/booksumo/

LEGAL NOTES

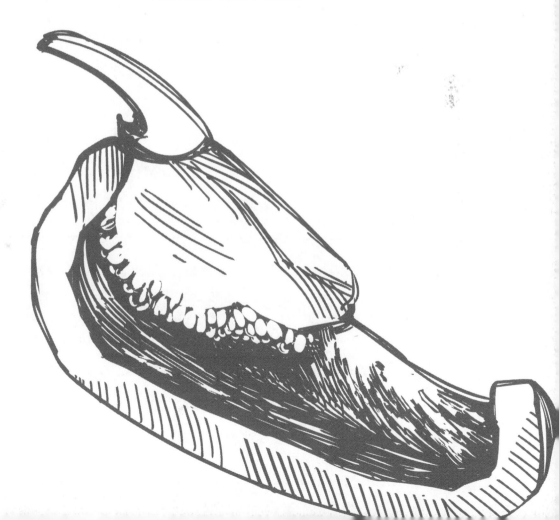

Table of Contents

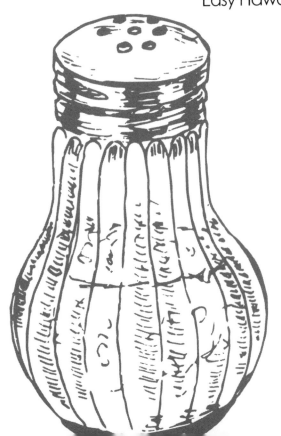
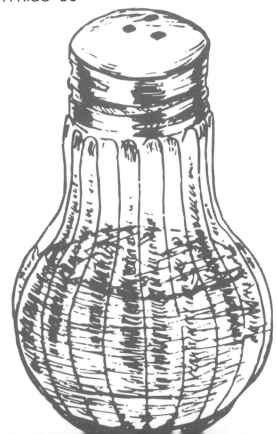

Creamy Mushrooms with Shrimp

🥄 Prep Time: 20 mins

🕐 Total Time: 35 mins

Servings per Recipe: 6	
Calories	317 kcal
Fat	6.3 g
Carbohydrates	43g
Protein	23.8 g
Cholesterol	173 mg
Sodium	1136 mg

Ingredients

2 C. instant brown rice
1 3/4 C. water
6 tbsps soy sauce
6 tbsps water
1/4 C. honey
2 tbsps cider vinegar
2 tbsps cornstarch
2 tbsps olive oil

2 cloves garlic, chopped
2 C. broccoli florets
1 C. baby carrots
1 small white onion, chopped
1/2 tsp black pepper
1 C. sliced fresh mushrooms
1 1/2 lbs uncooked medium shrimp, peeled and deveined

Directions

1. Get a bowl, mix: cornstarch, soy sauce, vinegar, honey, and water.
2. For 8 mins, in the microwave, cook your rice in 1 3/4 C. of water. Then stir it.
3. Stir fry your garlic in olive for 1 min then add in: black pepper, broccoli, onions, and carrots.
4. Continue frying for 7 more mins.
5. Then add the mushrooms and cook for 4 more mins.
6. Empty the pan.
7. Add in your cornstarch mix to the pan and cook it for 1.5 mins then add in your shrimp. Cook the shrimp for 4 mins before pouring in the veggies with the shrimp and reheating everything.
8. Serve the rice with the veggies and shrimp.
9. Enjoy.

GREENS, CORN, BLACK BEANS
and Olive Brown Rice

🥣 Prep Time: 10 mins
🕐 Total Time: 2 hr

Servings per Recipe: 24
Calories   87 kcal
Fat   1.7 g
Carbohydrates   16g
Protein   2.6 g
Cholesterol   0 mg
Sodium   340 mg

Ingredients

1 1/2 C. uncooked brown rice
3 C. water
1 tbsp extra virgin olive oil
1/2 tsp salt
1 (14.5 oz.) can collard greens, drained
1 (15 oz.) can black beans, rinsed and drained
1 (15 oz.) can green peas, rinsed and drained

1 (15.25 oz.) can corn kernels, drained
1 (4 oz.) can chopped green chilies
1 (4 oz.) can sliced black olives
1 (14.5 oz.) can Italian-style tomatoes, undrained and chopped
salt and freshly ground black pepper to taste

Directions

1. Boil: .5 tsp of salt, rice, olive oil, and water.
2. Once everything is boiling place a lid on the pan, set the heat to low, and let the contents cook for 17 mins.
3. Then pour everything into a bowl and stir.
4. Place the bowl in the fridge until room temp.
5. Once the rice is room temp add the following to it, then toss: pepper, collard greens, salt, beans, tomatoes, peas, olives, corn, and chilies.
6. Enjoy at room temp or slightly warm.

Cashews, Chickpeas and Mushroom Brown Rice (Pilaf I)

Prep Time: 10 mins
Total Time: 1 hr 20 mins

Servings per Recipe: 4
Calories   409 kcal
Fat   17.1 g
Carbohydrates   54g
Protein   12.5 g
Cholesterol   116 mg
Sodium   653 mg

Ingredients

1 1/2 C. water
1/2 tsp salt
3/4 C. uncooked brown rice
3 tbsps butter
1 1/2 C. chopped onion
1 clove garlic, minced
2 carrots, sliced

2 C. fresh sliced mushrooms
1 C. chickpeas
2 eggs, beaten
freshly ground black pepper
1/4 C. chopped fresh parsley
1/4 C. chopped cashews

Directions

1. Boil your rice in 1.5 C. of water for 47 mins, in a covered pot over low heat.
2. Halfway through the rice's cooking time, begin to stir fry your onions in butter until tender then combine in: carrots and garlic and fry for 6 more mins.
3. Add the mushrooms and cook for 11 mins before adding the chickpeas and frying for 2 more mins.
4. Cook your eggs in a pan after the rice is done and then add to them: nuts, parsley, and pepper.
5. Combine the rice with the eggs and also the veggies.
6. Serve everything topped with some soy sauce.
7. Enjoy.

BUTTERY AND BAKED
Brown Rice

🍲 Prep Time: 10 mins

🕐 Total Time: 1 hr 10 mins

Servings per Recipe: 6
Calories   206 kcal
Fat   5.1 g
Carbohydrates   36.2g
Protein   3.6 g
Cholesterol   10 mg
Sodium   420 mg

Ingredients

1 1/2 C. brown rice
1 tsp salt
2 tbsps butter
3 C. boiling water

Directions

1. Get your water boiling then set your oven to 400 degrees before doing anything else.
2. Now get a baking dish and add to it: butter, salt, and rice.
3. Top the mix with the boiling water and place a covering of foil over the dish.
4. Cook everything in the oven for 1 hr, then stir it.
5. Enjoy.

Instant Lemon and Parsley Brown Rice

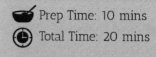 Prep Time: 10 mins
Total Time: 20 mins

Servings per Recipe: 4
Calories	109 kcal
Fat	3.6 g
Carbohydrates	16.8g
Protein	2.5 g
Cholesterol	8 mg
Sodium	24 mg

Ingredients

1 C. instant brown rice
1/2 tsp dried parsley
1/4 tsp ground black pepper
1 tbsp unsalted butter
1/2 tsp lemon juice
7 fluid oz. low-sodium chicken broth, or more if
needed

Directions

1. Get a measuring cup and add in: lemon juice, butter, and 7 oz. of broth.
2. Everything should equal exactly one 1 C.
3. Now get a bowl, add in: black pepper, the broth mix, parsley, and rice.
4. Place a lid on the bowl and cook it in the microwave for 8 mins.
5. Now remove the lid and let it cool for 7 mins before stirring.
6. Enjoy.

PEPPER, BALSAMIC, DIJON
and Raisins Brown Rice (Salad I)

🥣 Prep Time: 15 mins
🕐 Total Time: 1 hr

Servings per Recipe: 6

Calories	451 kcal
Fat	23.5 g
Carbohydrates	54.6g
Protein	7.1 g
Cholesterol	9 mg
Sodium	338 mg

Ingredients

1 1/2 C. uncooked brown rice
3 C. water
1 red bell pepper, thinly sliced
1 C. frozen green peas, thawed
1/2 C. raisins
1/4 sweet onion (such as Vidalia(R)), chopped
1/4 C. chopped Kalamata olives

1/2 C. vegetable oil
1/4 C. balsamic vinegar
1 1/4 tsps Dijon mustard
salt and ground black pepper to taste
1/4 C. feta cheese

Directions

1. Get your water and rice boiling, place a lid on the pot, set the heat to low, and let the contents cook, with a low heat, for 47 mins.
2. Get a bowl, mix: olives, bell pepper, onions, raisins, and peas.
3. Get a 2nd bowl, combine: mustard, vinegar, and veggie oil.
4. Combine both bowls then add in your ice and add some pepper and salt before adding in some cheese. Enjoy.

Peppers, Onions and Cheddar Brown Rice

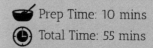 Prep Time: 10 mins

Total Time: 55 mins

Servings per Recipe: 8

Calories	95 kcal
Fat	1.5 g
Carbohydrates	15g
Protein	4.9 g
Cholesterol	3 mg
Sodium	87 mg

Ingredients

2 C. water
1 C. brown rice
1/2 red bell peppers, seeded and chopped
1/4 red onion, chopped
1 C. shredded low-fat Cheddar cheese

Directions

1. Get your water and rice boiling before placing a lid on the pot, setting the heat to low, and letting the contents cook for 47 mins.
2. Stir fry your onions and peppers in nonstick spray, until brown, and combine them with the rice, when it is finished.
3. Combine in your cheese and let it melt before plating the dish.
4. Enjoy.

EASY LATIN
Style Rice

🥣 Prep Time: 10 mins
🕐 Total Time: 1 hr 10 mins

Servings per Recipe: 4
Calories   156 kcal
Fat   1.3 g
Carbohydrates   32.3g
Protein   4 g
Cholesterol   2 mg
Sodium   1479 mg

Ingredients

1 (14 oz.) can chicken broth
1 (15 oz.) can diced tomatoes with green chili peppers
1 tsp salt
1 C. brown rice

Directions

1. Boil: rice, broth, salt, and tomatoes.
2. Once everything is boiling place a lid on the pot, set the heat to low, and cook the contents for 1 hr.
3. Let the rice cool for 7 mins before stirring it.
4. Enjoy.

Brown Rice
Risotto I

Prep Time: 30 mins
Total Time: 1 hr 30 mins

Servings per Recipe: 6
Calories	322 kcal
Fat	10.7 g
Carbohydrates	47.1g
Protein	10 g
Cholesterol	13 mg
Sodium	500 mg

Ingredients

1 quart vegetable broth, or as needed
5 C. water, or as needed
1/2 lb asparagus, cut into 2-inch pieces
2 tbsps olive oil
1 C. finely chopped onion
2 cloves garlic, finely chopped
2 C. short-grain brown rice

2 carrots, peeled and diced
2 zucchini, diced
1/2 C. green peas, thawed if frozen
2/3 C. grated Parmesan cheese
1 tbsp butter
salt and ground black pepper to taste

Directions

1. Boil your water and broth then add the asparagus to it and cook for 4 mins.
2. Place the veggies to the side in some cold water for 7 mins.
3. Now remove all the liquid from the bowl, place a lid on the boiling broth, and let it continue to boil.
4. Stir fry your garlic and onions in olive oil for 7 mins then add the rice and cook for 6 more mins.
5. Now add a half a C., at a time, of the hot broth, to the rice and stir until it is basically absorbed by the rice.
6. Continue doing this for about 20 mins.
7. Add in the carrots and continue adding liquid in batches for 20 more mins.
8. Now add in the zucchini, peas, and asparagus.
9. Cook everything for 5 more mins then combine in the butter and parmesan.
10. Once everything has melted add some pepper and salt and add .5 C. of broth as well.
11. Enjoy.

ZUCCHINI, CHICKEN, MUSHROOMS
and Swiss Brown Rice

Prep Time: 15 mins
Total Time: 1 hr 50 mins

Servings per Recipe: 8
Calories   337 kcal
Fat   21 g
Carbohydrates   11.5g
Protein   25.3 g
Cholesterol   77 mg
Sodium   363 mg

Ingredients

1/3 C. brown rice
1 C. vegetable broth
1 tbsp olive oil
1/3 C. diced onion
1 medium zucchini, thinly sliced
2 cooked skinless boneless chicken breast halves, chopped
1/2 C. sliced mushrooms

1/2 tsp cumin
salt to taste
ground cayenne pepper to taste
1 (15 oz.) can black beans, drained
1 (4 oz.) can diced green chile peppers, drained
1/3 C. shredded carrots
2 C. shredded Swiss cheese

Directions

1. Boil your broth and veggies, once everything is boiling place a lid on the pot, set the heat to low, and let the contents gently cook for 47 mins.
2. Coat a baking dish with oil and then set your oven to 350 degrees before doing anything else.
3. Stir fry your onions, until soft, in olive oil, for about 7 mins, then combine in: mushrooms, zucchini, and chicken along with some cayenne, cumin, and salt.
4. Stir fry the mix until the chicken is fully done.
5. Get a bowl, combine: half of the cheese, the rice, carrots, onions, chilies, zucchini, chilies, chicken, beans, and mushrooms.
6. Pour all the contents into the baking dish and cook it all in the oven covered with foil for 32 mins then take off the foil and cook for 8 more mins.
7. Let the casserole stand for 10 mins before plating.
8. Enjoy.

Meaty No-Meat
Brown Rice Bake

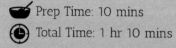 Prep Time: 10 mins

Total Time: 1 hr 10 mins

Servings per Recipe: 8

Calories	140 kcal
Fat	6.5 g
Carbohydrates	18.3g
Protein	2.2 g
Cholesterol	15 mg
Sodium	482 mg

Ingredients

1 C. brown rice
1 C. beef broth
1 (14.5 oz.) can chicken broth
1/4 C. butter, melted
1 tsp garlic salt
1 tsp seasoned salt

Directions

1. Set your oven to 350 degrees before doing anything else.
2. Get a baking dish and layer in it: rice, both broths, and butter.
3. Top with: seasoned salt and garlic salt.
4. Cook everything in the oven for 1 hr.
5. Enjoy.

EASY LOUISIANA
Style Brown Rice

🥣 Prep Time: 15 mins
🕐 Total Time: 1 hr 15 mins

Servings per Recipe: 4
Calories	495 kcal
Fat	25.2 g
Carbohydrates	37.3g
Protein	30.3 g
Cholesterol	221 mg
Sodium	1909 mg

Ingredients

2 tbsps butter
8 oz. andouille sausage, cut into 1/4-inch slices
2 tbsps ground paprika
1 tbsp ground cumin
1/2 tsp cayenne pepper
1/2 C. diced tomatoes
1 large green bell pepper, diced
2 stalks celery, sliced 1/4 inch thick

4 green onions, thinly sliced
1 tsp salt
1 bay leaf
1 C. uncooked brown rice
3 C. chicken stock
1 lb large shrimp, peeled and deveined
salt and ground black pepper to taste

Directions

1. Stir fry your sausage in butter, in a big pot, until browned.
2. Then add in: cayenne, cumin, and paprika.
3. Cook for 2 more mins.
4. Now combine in: salt, bay leaf, tomatoes, onions, pepper, and celery.
5. Stir the contents and cook for 1 more min before adding the stock and rice.
6. Get everything boiling and once it is boiling place a lid on the pot, set the heat to low, and let the contents cook for 47 mins.
7. Add in the shrimp and let them cook for 7 mins before adding in some pepper and salt.
8. Enjoy.

Easy Mexican
Style Brown Rice

🥣 Prep Time: 20 mins
🕐 Total Time: 1 hr 20 mins

Servings per Recipe: 10
Calories   124 kcal
Fat   1 g
Carbohydrates   26g
Protein   4.7 g
Cholesterol   0 mg
Sodium   220 mg

Ingredients

1 C. brown rice
1 C. beef broth
1 (14.5 oz.) can chicken broth
1/4 C. butter, melted
1 tsp garlic salt
1 tsp seasoned salt

Directions

1. Get a bowl, combine: cumin, rice, garlic, beans, cilantro, corn, lime juice & zest, onions, jalapenos, and green peppers.
2. Add in your preferred amount of pepper and salt and place the contents in the fridge for 60 mins then stir everything and serve.
3. Enjoy.

BLACK BEAN
and Rice Burgers (Vegetarian Approved)

Prep Time: 25 mins
Total Time: 41 mins

Servings per Recipe: 6
Calories	317 kcal
Fat	5.8 g
Carbohydrates	49.4g
Protein	18.2 g
Cholesterol	71 mg
Sodium	1704 mg

Ingredients

1/2 C. uncooked brown rice
1 C. water
2 (16 oz.) cans black beans, rinsed and drained
1 green bell pepper, halved and seeded
1 onion, quartered
1/2 C. sliced mushrooms
6 cloves garlic, peeled
3/4 C. shredded mozzarella cheese

2 eggs
1 tbsp chili powder
1 tbsp ground cumin
1 tbsp garlic salt
1 tsp hot sauce
1/2 C. dry bread crumbs, or as needed

Directions

1. Get your water and rice boiling, then place a lid on the pot, set the heat to low, and let the contents gently cook for 47 mins.
2. Heat up your grill and cover the grate with foil.
3. With a blender, process: garlic, bell pepper, mushrooms, and onions. Then place everything in a bowl.
4. Now blend the mozzarella and the rice and add them to the same bowl
5. Get a 2nd bowl, mash: black beans until paste like.
6. Then add in the blended mix.
7. Get a 3rb bowl, combine: beaten eggs, hot sauce, chili powder, garlic salt, and cumin.
8. Add this to the beans and then mix in your bread crumbs.
9. Shape the bean mix into 6 burgers then grill each for 7 mins per side.
10. Enjoy the patties with sesame seed buns and some mayo.
11. Enjoy.

Walnuts, Broccoli and Cheddar Brown Rice

🥣 Prep Time: 15 mins
🕐 Total Time: 40 mins

Servings per Recipe: 4	
Calories	368 kcal
Fat	22.9 g
Carbohydrates	30.4g
Protein	15.1 g
Cholesterol	37 mg
Sodium	643 mg

Ingredients

1/2 C. chopped walnuts
1 tbsp butter
1 onion, chopped
1/2 tsp minced garlic
1 C. uncooked instant brown rice
1 C. vegetable broth
1 lb fresh broccoli florets

1/2 tsp salt
1/8 tsp ground black pepper
1 C. shredded Cheddar cheese

Directions

1. Set your oven to 350 degrees before doing anything else.
2. Get a baking dish and toast your nuts in the oven for 9 mins.
3. Microwave the broccoli until soft, then add in some pepper and salt.
4. Now stir fry your garlic and onions in butter for 4 mins then add in the broth and rice. Get everything boiling, then place a lid on the pot, and let the contents, gently cook over a lower level of heat for 9 mins.
5. On each serving plate add a layer of rice, then some broccoli, then nuts, and finally some cheese.
6. Enjoy.

BUTTERY PARSLEY
and Shrimp

Prep Time: 15 mins
Total Time: 35 mins

Servings per Recipe: 4
Calories	551 kcal
Fat	23 g
Carbohydrates	40.2g
Protein	38.5 g
Cholesterol	282 mg
Sodium	322 mg

Ingredients

1 C. brown rice
1 2/3 C. water
3 tbsps butter
3 tbsps olive oil
2 cloves garlic, minced
1/2 C. white wine
2 tbsps fresh lemon juice
1 1/2 lbs medium shrimp - peeled and deveined

1/4 C. chopped fresh flat-leaf parsley
1/2 tsp cornstarch

Directions

1. Boil your water and rice. Once everything is boiling set the heat to low, and let the contents gently cook for 27 mins.
2. Stir fry your garlic in butter for 4 mins then add the lemon juice and wine.
3. Get the mix simmering then pour in the shrimp and cook for 8 mins. Now top everything with parsley and cook for 3 more mins.
4. Grab your cornstarch and gradually pour it in while stirring and cooking for about 1 to 2 mins until you have made a thick sauce.
5. Place your rice on a plate then top with the shrimp and sauce.
6. Enjoy.

Onions, Chicken, Peas and Garlic Brown Rice

Prep Time: 20 mins
Total Time: 35 mins

Servings per Recipe: 3

Calories	486 kcal
Fat	13.7 g
Carbohydrates	57.4g
Protein	32.1 g
Cholesterol	64 mg
Sodium	720 mg

Ingredients

2 tbsps vegetable oil, divided
8 oz. skinless, boneless chicken breast, cut into strips
1/2 red bell pepper, chopped
1/2 C. green onion, chopped
4 cloves garlic, minced
3 C. cooked brown rice
2 tbsps light soy sauce
1 tbsp rice vinegar
1 C. frozen peas, thawed

Directions

1. Stir fry your garlic, chicken, onions, and bell peppers in half of the veggie oil for 7 mins or until the chicken is fully done.
2. Place the chicken mix to the side.
3. Add in the rest of the oil and toast your rice in it for 1 min then add: peas, vinegar, and soy sauce.
4. Cook for 2 more mins and add back in the chicken.
5. Once everything is heated through you can serve it.
6. Enjoy.

EASY INDIAN STYLE
Brown Rice with Chicken

Prep Time: 15 mins
Total Time: 1 hr 15 mins

Servings per Recipe: 4
Calories	241 kcal
Fat	2 g
Carbohydrates	34.5g
Protein	22.7 g
Cholesterol	50 mg
Sodium	620 mg

Ingredients

1 C. water
1 (8 oz.) can stewed tomatoes
3/4 C. quick-cooking brown rice
1/2 C. raisins
1 tbsp lemon juice
3 tsps curry powder
1 cube chicken bouillon
1/2 tsp ground cinnamon

1/4 tsp salt
2 cloves garlic, minced
1 bay leaf (optional)
3/4 lb skinless, boneless chicken breast halves -
cut into 1 inch pieces

Directions

1. Set your oven to 350 degrees before doing anything else.
2. Boil the following for 2 mins: bay leaf, water, garlic, tomatoes, salt, brown rice, cinnamon, raisins, bouillon, lemon juice, and curry.
3. Now add in the chicken, and cook for 2 more mins before pouring everything into a baking dish.
4. Place a covering of foil around the dish and cook the contents in the oven for 47 mins stirring everything half way through the cooking time. Enjoy.

Balsamic Cranberries and Onions Brown Rice

Prep Time: 15 mins
Total Time: 3 hr 15 mins

Servings per Recipe: 4	
Calories	302 kcal
Fat	10.3 g
Carbohydrates	49.7g
Protein	3.8 g
Cholesterol	0 mg
Sodium	365 mg

Ingredients

2 C. water
1 C. brown rice
1/4 C. diced red onion
1/2 C. diced celery
1/4 C. dried cranberries
1/2 C. balsamic vinaigrette salad dressing
1 tbsp sugar

Directions

1. Boil your water then add in the rice, place a lid on the pot, and let the contents gently cook with a low level of heat for 47 mins.
2. Let everything cool for 5 mins, then stir, and place it all in a bowl.
3. Add to the rice: sugar, onions, vinaigrette, celery, and cranberries.
4. Place some plastic wrap around the bowl, and let everything chill in the fridge for 30 mins before serving.
5. Enjoy.

MAPLE ALMONDS
and Raisins Brown Rice
(Breakfast I)

Prep Time: 15 mins
Total Time: 20 mins

Servings per Recipe: 4
Calories   406 kcal
Fat   11.6 g
Carbohydrates   68.9g
Protein   10.2 g
Cholesterol   0 mg
Sodium   44 mg

Ingredients

1 C. water
3 C. cooked brown rice
1/2 C. raisins
1/4 C. real maple syrup
1 C. soy milk
1/2 C. toasted and chopped almonds
1 tsp ground cinnamon
1/2 tsp ground cardamom

Directions

1. Get the following boiling: cardamom, rice, cinnamon, raisins, almond, syrup, and almonds.
2. Once everything is boiling set the heat to low and let the contents gently cook for 9 mins.
3. Before serving, let the dish, loose some of its heat for 5 mins. Enjoy.

Easy
Blueberry Porridge (Breakfast II)

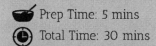 Prep Time: 5 mins

Total Time: 30 mins

Servings per Recipe: 2	
Calories	318 kcal
Fat	11.6 g
Carbohydrates	44.7g
Protein	9.9 g
Cholesterol	118 mg
Sodium	130 mg

Ingredients

1 C. cooked brown rice
1 C. 2% low-fat milk
2 tbsps dried blueberries
1 dash cinnamon
1 tbsp honey
1 egg
1/4 tsp vanilla extract

1 tbsp butter

Directions

1. Get the following boiling: honey, rice, cinnamon, berries, and milk.
2. Once everything is boiling set the heat to low and let the contents gently cook for 22 mins.
3. Get a bowl and whisk the egg in it then add in some rice one tbsp at a time until you have adding in six tbsps.
4. Now add some butter and vanilla to your rice and then pour in the egg mix.
5. Cook for 3 more mins before shutting the heat and serving. Enjoy.

BLACK BEANS, CORN
and Salsa Brown Rice

🥄 Prep Time: 10 mins

🕐 Total Time: 41 mins

Servings per Recipe: 8
Calories   521 kcal
Fat   22.4 g
Carbohydrates   41.8g
Protein   30.8 g
Cholesterol   91 mg
Sodium   1129 mg

Ingredients

2 1/2 tbsps Taco Seasoning
1 lb boneless skinless chicken thighs, cut into bite-size pieces
2 tbsps Italian Dressing
1 C. canned black beans
1/2 C. frozen corn
2 green onions, chopped
1 C. Salsa

1/2 C. Shredded Four Cheese
2 2/3 C. hot cooked long-grain brown rice

Directions

1. Set your oven to 375 degrees before doing anything else.
2. Get a bowl, combine: chicken and taco spice.
3. Now stir fry your seasoned chicken in dressing for about 7 mins then pour it all into a baking dish.
4. Layer the following over the chicken: salt, beans, onions, and corn.
5. Cook the casserole in the oven for 22 mins then add some cheese and cook everything for 4 more mins.
6. Enjoy the dish with rice.

Celery, Onions, Walnuts and Mushrooms Brown Rice

Prep Time: 10 mins
Total Time: 40 mins

Servings per Recipe: 8
Calories   163 kcal
Fat   9.1 g
Carbohydrates   19.7g
Protein   3.4 g
Cholesterol   1 mg
Sodium   227 mg

Ingredients

2 tbsps olive oil
1 small onion, chopped
1/4 C. celery, chopped
1 1/2 C. sliced mushrooms
1 (14.5 oz.) can chicken broth
2 C. Minute(R) Brown Rice, uncooked
1/2 C. chopped walnuts, toasted

2 tbsps fresh parsley, chopped

Directions

1. Stir fry for 5 mins your celery and onions in oil. Then add in the mushrooms and cook for 4 more mins.
2. Pour in the broth and get everything boiling.
3. Once everything is boiling pour in the rice and get it boiling again, now place a lid on the pot and let the content gently cook with a low level of heat for 5 mins.
4. Shut the heat and let it cool for 7 mins then add in some parsley and walnuts.
5. Enjoy.

CILANTRO AND CORN
Brown Rice

Prep Time: 5 mins
Total Time: 1 hr 5 mins

Servings per Recipe: 6
Calories   133 kcal
Fat   3.2 g
Carbohydrates   24.4g
Protein   2.7 g
Cholesterol   0 mg
Sodium   198 mg

Ingredients

2 C. water
1 C. brown rice
1 tbsp olive oil
1/2 tsp salt
1 C. frozen corn kernels
1/2 tsp dried cilantro
1/2 tsp cumin seed

Directions

1. Get the following boiling: salt, water, olive oil, and rice.
2. Once everything is boiling add in: cumin, cilantro, and corn.
3. Set the heat to low, place a lid on the pot, and let the mix gently cook for 50 mins.
4. Before serving, stir the rice after it has cooled off.
5. Enjoy.

Easy African
Style Brown Rice

Prep Time: 30 mins

Total Time: 5 hr 30 mins

Servings per Recipe: 20	
Calories	205 kcal
Fat	8.7 g
Carbohydrates	22.8g
Protein	10.8 g
Cholesterol	14 mg
Sodium	353 mg

Ingredients

2 tbsps olive oil
2 large skinless, boneless chicken breast halves
1 onion, chopped
2 red bell peppers, sliced
4 cloves garlic, minced
1 (28 oz.) can crushed tomatoes
2 sweet potatoes, peeled and cut into bite-size pieces
3 C. sliced carrots
4 C. chicken broth, or more as needed

1/2 tsp curry powder
1/2 tsp ground cumin
1/4 tsp chili powder
1/4 tsp cayenne pepper
1/4 tsp crushed red pepper flakes
1/4 tsp ground cinnamon
1/4 tsp ground black pepper
1 C. brown rice
1 C. crunchy peanut butter

Directions

1. For 6 mins, per side, fry your chicken in olive oil.
2. Put everything in your crock pot.
3. Now in the same pan stir fry: garlic, bell pepper, and onions for 7 mins then add it to the crock pot as well.
4. Also add the following to the crock pot: black pepper, tomatoes, cinnamon, sweet potatoes, red pepper, carrots, cayenne, broth, chili powder, curry, and cumin.
5. Cook for 10 hrs. with a low heat.
6. Now add the rice when 3 hrs. are left in the cooking time.
7. Once 60 mins is left add the peanut butter.
8. Shred the chicken after everything is done then pour the shredded meat back into the slow cooker.
9. Enjoy.

RED
Lentil Burgers: (Vegetarian Approved)

Prep Time: 20 mins
Total Time: 40 mins

Servings per Recipe: 16

Calories	242 kcal
Fat	8.3 g
Carbohydrates	30.3g
Protein	11.2 g
Cholesterol	27 mg
Sodium	395 mg

Ingredients

2 tbsps vegetable oil
3/4 C. uncooked brown rice
1 1/2 C. red lentils
6 C. water
1 tsp salt
2 eggs
2 1/2 C. dry bread crumbs
1 1/2 C. grated Parmesan cheese

2 tsps dried basil
1 1/2 tsps garlic powder
3 tbsps vegetable oil

Directions

1. Toast your rice in olive oil until brown and then add in the water, salt, and lentils.
2. Get the mix boiling, then place a lid on the pot, set the heat to low, and cook for 42 mins.
3. Let the rice mix loose most of its heat then blend it in a blender or food processor with: garlic powder, eggs, basil, bread crumbs, basil, and parmesan.
4. Blend everything until you find that the mix has a meat like consistency.
5. Then shape the mix into patties.
6. With a batch process, fry the patties, in 3 tbsps of olive oil, for 3 mins each side.
7. Now place them on paper towels to drain off the excess oils.
8. You can freeze these patties and then reheat them in the microwave or store everything in the fridge.
9. Enjoy.

Authentic
Enchiladas

Prep Time: 15 mins
Total Time: 1 hr 5 mins

Servings per Recipe: 8
Calories   322 kcal
Fat   11 g
Carbohydrates   44.4g
Protein   12.8 g
Cholesterol   19 mg
Sodium   994 mg

Ingredients

1 tbsp olive oil
1 green bell pepper, chopped
1 onion, chopped
3 cloves garlic, minced
1 (15 oz.) can black beans, rinsed and drained
1 (14.5 oz.) can diced tomatoes and green chilies
1/4 C. picante sauce
1 tbsp chili powder

1 tsp ground cumin
1/4 tsp red pepper flakes
2 C. cooked brown rice
8 (6 inch) flour tortillas, warmed
1 C. salsa
1 C. shredded Cheddar cheese
3 tbsps chopped fresh cilantro leaves
1/4 C. shredded Cheddar cheese

Directions

1. Coat a casserole dish with oil and then set your oven to 350 degrees before doing anything else.
2. Stir fry your: garlic, onions, and green peppers in oil for 9 mins then add: pepper flakes, beans, cumin, tomatoes, chili powder, and picante sauce. Get this boiling then set the heat to low and cook for 7 mins.
3. Add the rice and cheddar and cook for 7 more mins with no lid.
4. Add half a C. of this mix to the middle of each of your tortillas then shape each one into enchiladas.
5. With the seam facing downwards place each enchilada into your casserole dish and top with salsa.
6. Place a wrapping of foil around the dish cook everything in the oven for 27 mins.
7. Remove the wrapping and top your dish with: a quarter of a C. of cheddar, and some cilantro.
8. Cook for 4 more mins.
9. Let the enchiladas sit for 7 mins before serving.
10. Enjoy.

ONIONS, GINGER and Raisins Brown Rice

🥣 Prep Time: 10 mins
🕐 Total Time: 55 mins

Servings per Recipe: 7	
Calories	161 kcal
Fat	4.5 g
Carbohydrates	28.2g
Protein	2.7 g
Cholesterol	4 mg
Sodium	95 mg

Ingredients

1 C. brown rice
2 C. chicken broth
1 tbsp butter
1 bay leaf
1 tbsp vegetable oil
1 C. chopped onion
1 tsp minced fresh ginger
1 tsp ground cumin

1/2 tsp ground coriander
1/3 C. thinly sliced celery
1/4 C. seedless raisins
1 tbsp low-sodium soy sauce
freshly ground black pepper to taste

Directions

1. Boil your rice in broth and butter with a bay leaf.
2. Once everything is boiling, place a lid on the pot, set the heat to low, and gently cook for 37 mins.
3. At the same time stir fry your ginger and onions in veggie oil for 5 mins then add in coriander, celery, cumin, and raisins.
4. Cook for 6 more mins.
5. Combine the raisin mix with the rice and stir to evenly distribute everything throughout the rice.
6. Add your preferred amount of pepper and salt and also add in the soy sauce before serving.
7. Enjoy.

Peppers, Kidney Beans
Mushrooms, and Almonds Brown Rice

Prep Time: 20 mins
Total Time: 2 hr 30 mins

Servings per Recipe: 6	
Calories	223 kcal
Fat	4.5 g
Carbohydrates	39.2g
Protein	7.1 g
Cholesterol	0 mg
Sodium	203 mg

Ingredients

1 C. uncooked brown rice
1 1/2 C. water
1 (15 oz.) can kidney beans, rinsed and drained
1/4 C. chopped red onion
1/4 C. sliced fresh mushrooms
1/4 C. bite-size broccoli florets
1/4 C. chopped green bell pepper

1/4 C. chopped red bell pepper
1/4 C. chopped yellow bell pepper
2 tbsps raw almonds
1/4 tsp coarse black pepper
2 tbsps fat free Italian-style dressing
1 tbsp extra-virgin olive oil

Directions

1. Set your oven to 350 degrees before doing anything else.
2. Place your almonds in a casserole dish and toast them in the oven until aromatic for about 5 to 9 mins.
3. Once toasted and brown place them in a blender and blend them down into little chunks. Place everything to the side.
4. Boil your water and rice, then place a lid on the pot, set the heat to low, and let the contents gently cook for 47 mins.
5. Get a bowl, combine: pepper, rice, blended almonds, kidney beans, bell peppers, onions, broccoli, and mushrooms.
6. Add in your olive oil and dressing and then stir everything.
7. Place the bowl in the fridge for 30 mins until chilled.
8. Enjoy.

EASY GREEK
Style Brown Rice

🥣 Prep Time: 20 mins
🕐 Total Time: 2 hr

Servings per Recipe: 8

Calories	224 kcal
Fat	12.7 g
Carbohydrates	24.6g
Protein	4.5 g
Cholesterol	8 mg
Sodium	304 mg

Ingredients

1 C. uncooked long grain brown rice
2 1/2 C. water
1 avocado - peeled, pitted, and diced
1/4 C. lemon juice
2 vine-ripened tomatoes, diced
1 1/2 C. diced English cucumbers
1/3 C. diced red onion
1/2 C. crumbled feta cheese

1/4 C. sliced Kalamata olives
1/4 C. chopped fresh mint
3 tbsps olive oil
1 tsp lemon zest
1/2 tsp minced garlic
1/2 tsp kosher salt
1/2 tsp ground black pepper

Directions

1. Boil your water and rice, then place a lid on the pot, set the heat to low, and let the contents gently cook for 47 mins.
2. Once everything is cool, stir the rice.
3. Get a bowl, combine: pepper, avocado, salt, lemon juice, garlic, tomatoes, lemon zest, cucumber, olive oil, onions, mint, olives, and feta.
4. Now add in your rice and stir the entire mix before placing a covering of plastic around the bowl and putting the bowl in the fridge to chill for 60 mins before serving. Enjoy.

Easy Jamaican
Style Brown Rice

Prep Time: 15 mins
Total Time: 45 mins

Servings per Recipe: 2
Calories   398 kcal
Fat   10.7 g
Carbohydrates   71.6g
Protein   6.1 g
Cholesterol   0 mg
Sodium   11 mg

Ingredients

1 tbsp vegetable oil
1/2 large onion, sliced
1/2 red apple, cored and sliced
1 pinch curry powder
1 C. water
2/3 C. brown rice
1 tsp dark molasses or treacle

1 small banana, sliced
1 tbsp unsweetened flaked coconut

Directions

1. Stir fry your apples and onions in oil until the onions are see-through then add in curry.
2. Cook everything for 1 more min before pouring in your water, molasses, and rice.
3. Get everything boiling before placing a lid on the pot, setting the heat to low, and cooking for 32 mins.
4. Add in the bananas and then your coconuts. Get everything hot again then plate the rice.
5. Enjoy.

EASY INDIAN STYLE
Brown Rice II

🥣 Prep Time: 15 mins
🕐 Total Time: 55 mins

Servings per Recipe: 4
Calories	225 kcal
Fat	10.1 g
Carbohydrates	30.7g
Protein	3.5 g
Cholesterol	23 mg
Sodium	407 mg

Ingredients

3 tbsps butter
1/2 onion, minced
2 cloves garlic, minced
2 C. chicken stock
1 C. brown rice
1 tsp curry powder
1/4 tsp ground turmeric
1/2 tsp dried thyme

1 bay leaf

Directions

1. Stir fry your garlic and onions in butter for 7 mins.
2. Add your broth to a large pot and get it boiling,
3. Once everything is boiling add your rice and: bay leaf, garlic & onions, curry powder, thyme, and turmeric.
4. Place a lid on the pot, set the heat to low, and let the contents gently cook for 42 mins.
5. Let the rice cool before stirring it, then plate. Enjoy.

Honey, Oranges, Spinach and Balsamic Brown Rice

Prep Time: 10 mins
Total Time: 1 hr 50 mins

Servings per Recipe: 4
Calories   425 kcal
Fat   9 g
Carbohydrates   80.8g
Protein   7 g
Cholesterol   0 mg
Sodium   311 mg

Ingredients

1 1/2 C. uncooked brown rice
3 C. water
2/3 C. orange juice
2 tbsps vegetable oil
2 tbsps balsamic vinegar
2 tbsps honey
2 tsps orange zest

1/2 tsp salt
1 1/2 C. spinach leaves, packed
2 large orange, peeled, sectioned, and cut into bite-size
1/3 C. slivered red onion

Directions

1. Get your water and rice boiling, then place a lid on the pot, and let the contents cook with a low level of heat for 47 mins.
2. At the same time get a bowl, and mix in it: salt, orange zest & juice, oil, honey, and balsamic.
3. Once the rice has finished cooking top it with the dressing mix and place everything in the fridge covered with plastic wrap and let the contents chill for 30 mins.
4. Add your onions and spinach before plating the rice.
5. Enjoy.

MUSHROOM
Loaf (Vegetarian Approved)

Prep Time: 45 mins
Total Time: 1 hr 55 mins

Servings per Recipe: 6
Calories	384 kcal
Fat	12.8 g
Carbohydrates	59.3g
Protein	16 g
Cholesterol	0 mg
Sodium	468 mg

Ingredients

1 tbsp olive oil
12 oz. Crimini mushrooms, chopped
1 small red onion, finely diced
1 red bell pepper, seeded and diced
1 tbsp ground sage
1 1/4 C. cooked brown rice
1/2 C. walnuts, finely chopped
1 envelope onion soup mix

1 C. oat bran
1 C. wheat germ
2 egg whites, lightly beaten
1 tsp Worcestershire sauce
2 tsps prepared mustard

Directions

1. Coat a bread pan with oil or nonstick spray and then set your oven to 350 degrees before doing anything else.
2. Stir fry your: bell peppers, onions, and mushrooms for 7 mins in olive oil then add in some sage and cook for 6 more mins. Then pour everything into a bowl.
3. Combine in the bowl, the following: mustard, rice, Worcestershire, nuts, eggs whites, soup mix, wheat germ, and oat bran.
4. Pack everything into your bread pan and make sure the top is flat before cooking the loaf in the oven for 60 mins.
5. Cool the mix for 13 mins before cutting the loaf for serving.
6. Enjoy.

Cinnamon and Almonds Brown Rice (Breakfast III)

🥣 Prep Time: 5 mins

🕐 Total Time: 2 hr 5 mins

Servings per Recipe: 8	
Calories	326 kcal
Fat	5.8 g
Carbohydrates	61g
Protein	8 g
Cholesterol	19 mg
Sodium	298 mg

Ingredients

4 C. water
2 C. uncooked brown rice
3/4 tsp salt
2 C. milk
1 (12 fluid oz.) can evaporated milk
1/2 tsp almond extract
1 C. sugar

1 (3 inch) piece cinnamon stick

Directions

1. Get your rice boiling in water then add in your salt, place a lid on the pot, set the heat to low, and cook for 47 mins.
2. Add the following to the rice: sugar, the cinnamon stick, regular milk, extract, and evaporated milk.
3. Take the lid off of the pot and cook for 1 hr. more. Enjoy.

GREEN BEANS, ASPARAGUS
and Cheddar Brown Rice

Prep Time: 15 mins
Total Time: 1 hr 45 mins

Servings per Recipe: 12

Calories	238 kcal
Fat	10 g
Carbohydrates	19.1g
Protein	17.5 g
Cholesterol	47 mg
Sodium	714 mg

Ingredients

2 (10.75 oz.) cans condensed cream of asparagus soup
10 3/4 fluid oz. milk
1 1/2 C. water
1 lb chopped cooked chicken
1 C. uncooked brown rice
2 (14.5 oz.) cans French cut green beans
1 1/2 C. shredded Cheddar cheese

1 C. chopped onion
3 cloves garlic, crushed
1 tbsp dried parsley
1 1/2 tsps dried basil
1 tsp dried dill weed
salt and pepper to taste

Directions

1. Coat a baking dish with oil or nonstick spray and then set your oven to 375 degrees before doing anything else.
2. Get a bowl, combine: pepper, soup, salt, milk, dill, water, basil, chicken, parsley, rice, garlic, beans, onions, and cheese.
3. Pour everything into your dish and then cook the contents in the oven for 90 mins.
4. Also if the mix gets too dry during its cooking, feel free to add more water.
5. Enjoy.

Lime and Garlic
Brown Rice

🥣 Prep Time: 10 mins
🕐 Total Time: 45 mins

Servings per Recipe: 4
Calories   359 kcal
Fat   3.8 g
Carbohydrates   73.6g
Protein   7.3 g
Cholesterol   0 mg
Sodium   454 mg

Ingredients

4 C. water
2 C. brown rice
1 lime, juiced
1 tsp minced garlic
1 tsp extra-virgin olive oil
1 tsp sea salt
1/2 C. chopped fresh cilantro

Directions

1. Get your rice and water boiling, then place a lid on the pot, and let the contents cook for 47 mins over a lower level of heat.
2. After the rice has cooked, let it cool a bit, then stir it before pouring it all into a bowl.
3. Get a 2nd bowl, add: salt, lime juice, cilantro, olive oil, and garlic.
4. Stir everything nicely then mix it all with the rice.
5. Plate your rice.
6. Enjoy.

EASY THAI
Style Brown Rice

Prep Time: 30 mins
Total Time: 1 hr

Servings per Recipe: 6
Calories	644 kcal
Fat	35.4 g
Carbohydrates	51.6g
Protein	34.7 g
Cholesterol	52 mg
Sodium	689 mg

Ingredients

1 1/2 tbsps grated ginger
2 cucumbers, cut in half lengthwise, then into .5 in pieces.
1/3 C. vegetable oil
1 1/2 tbsps sugar
1 1/2 tbsps garlic, minced
1/2 C. red onion, finely chopped
6 oz. fresh spinach, cut into strips

3 C. cooked chicken, cut into 1/2-inch cubes
1/2 C. fresh basil, cut into strips
3/4 C. peanut butter
1/2 C. rice vinegar
1/2 poblano chili, seeded and chopped
1/3 C. lite soy sauce
1 1/2 C. Brown Rice

Directions

1. Get your rice boiling in the water, place a lid on the pot, set the heat to low, and simmer everything for 47 mins or until you find that the rice is tender.
2. Let the rice loose some of its heat then stir with a fork and add it to a bowl.
3. Get a 2nd bowl, combine: poblanos, peanut butter, garlic, vinegar, ginger, oil, sugar, and soy sauce.
4. Add the cucumbers with your rice and then add onions, chicken, and mix everything.
5. Now top the cucumber mix with the contents of the 2nd bowl.
6. Add some basil and spinach before plating the rice.
7. Enjoy.

Easy
Stuff Peppers

Prep Time: 20 mins
Total Time: 55 mins

Servings per Recipe: 6

Calories	230 kcal
Fat	6.5 g
Carbohydrates	33.4g
Protein	10.7 g
Cholesterol	18 mg
Sodium	309 mg

Ingredients

1 1/4 C. water
1 (3 oz.) package reduced-fat cream cheese, softened
2 C. cooked brown rice
2 C. chopped fresh spinach
1 (10 oz.) can diced tomatoes with green chili peppers
1 (15 oz.) can no-salt-added black beans, drained and rinsed

2 tbsps dried minced onion
1 tsp ground cumin
1 tsp dried oregano
3 large bell peppers, cut in half, with stems discarded
1/2 C. shredded Cheddar cheese

Directions

1. Set your oven to 350 degrees before doing anything else.
2. Get a casserole dish and add in some water.
3. Get a bowl, mix: oregano, brown rice, cumin, spinach, diced tomatoes, onions, beans, and cream cheese.
4. Divide the mix between your peppers and stuff them.
5. Layer everything in your dish and top with the cheese.
6. Cook everything in the oven for 40 mins.
7. Enjoy.

RUSTIC STYLE
Brown Rice

🍲 Prep Time: 10 mins
🕐 Total Time: 1 hr 25 mins

Servings per Recipe: 10
Calories	190 kcal
Fat	10.6 g
Carbohydrates	20.1g
Protein	4.5 g
Cholesterol	10 mg
Sodium	327 mg

Ingredients

cooking spray
2 1/2 C. chicken broth
1 1/2 C. brown and wild rice mix
3 tbsps butter
1 C. slivered almonds
2 tbsps dried parsley
1 C. sweetened dried cranberries
1/4 tsp salt

1/4 tsp ground black pepper

Directions

1. Coat a casserole dish with nonstick spray and then set your oven to 375 degrees.
2. Add your rice to the casserole dish then top with broth which was previously boiling.
3. Place a wrapping of foil around the dish and cook everything in the oven for 60 mins.
4. Stir fry your almonds in butter for 6 mins then add in some parsley and cook for 4 more mins.
5. Get a bowl, combine: pepper, baked rice, salt, almond mix, and berries together then plate the mix for serving.
6. Enjoy.

Sage and Black Bean Brown Rice

Prep Time: 15 mins
Total Time: 1 hr 55 mins

Servings per Recipe: 10	
Calories	101 kcal
Fat	1.2 g
Carbohydrates	15.4g
Protein	6.8 g
Cholesterol	14 mg
Sodium	759 mg

Ingredients

5 C. chicken broth
2 skinless, boneless chicken breast halves
1 C. diced celery
1 C. diced onion
1/4 C. diced carrots
1/4 C. corn
1/4 C. drained and rinsed black beans

1 tsp dried sage
1 tsp ground black pepper
1 tsp salt
1 bay leaf
3/4 C. brown rice

Directions

1. Get your broth boiling and cook the chicken in it for 22 mins.
2. Then place the chicken to the side before shredding it.
3. Add the following to the boiling broth: bay leaves, chicken, salt, rice, celery, pepper, onions, sage, carrots, black beans, and corn.
4. Let the contents continue to cook for 60 more mins. Then serve after letting it sit for 12 to 15 mins.
5. Enjoy.

EASY
Moroccan Style Brown Rice

🥣 Prep Time: 15 mins
🕐 Total Time: 1 hr 30 mins

Servings per Recipe: 6
Calories	681 kcal
Fat	23.1 g
Carbohydrates	82.2g
Protein	36.6 g
Cholesterol	97 mg
Sodium	1425 mg

Ingredients

1/2 C. soy sauce
1/2 C. fresh lemon juice
1/2 C. sherry
1/2 C. honey
1/2 tsp ground thyme
2 tsps curry powder
1/2 tsp dried oregano
1/2 tsp ground ginger

1/2 tsp ground black pepper
1 clove garlic, pressed
3 lbs cut up chicken pieces
1 1/2 C. uncooked brown rice
3 C. water
2 tbsps olive oil
8 pitted prunes
8 dried apricot halves

Directions

1. Place your chicken in a bowl with the following: garlic, soy sauce, black pepper, lemon juice, ginger, sherry, oregano, honey, curry, and thyme.
2. Place a covering of plastic wrap around the bowl and marinate it in the fridge for 60 mins to overnight (longer is better).
3. Get your water and rice boiling, then place a lid on the pot, let the contents cook for 47 mins with a low level of heat.
4. Stir fry your chicken in olive oil until fully browned then add in apricots and prunes.
5. Cook for 1 more min before pouring in the marinade.
6. Let the contents lightly boil with a low to medium level of heat until the chicken is fully done for about 17 mins.
7. Enjoy the rice with a topping of chicken.

NOTE: Check the internal temp. of the chicken to ensure that it is at least 160 degrees Fahrenheit.

Peppers and Honey
Brown Rice

Prep Time: 20 mins
Total Time: 2 hr 20 mins

Servings per Recipe: 8
Calories	203 kcal
Fat	6.9 g
Carbohydrates	30.5g
Protein	5.5 g
Cholesterol	14 mg
Sodium	143 mg

Ingredients

1 2/3 C. uncooked brown rice
2 1/2 C. water
1 C. low fat sour cream
1 tbsp red wine vinegar
1 tbsp fresh lime juice
2 tsps honey
1/2 tsp ground cumin
1/4 tsp chili powder

1/4 tsp salt
1/8 tsp black pepper
2 slices bacon
1 C. diced red bell pepper
1 C. chopped green onions
1/2 C. frozen green peas, thawed
1/4 C. toasted almond slices
2 tbsps chopped cilantro

Directions

1. Boil your water and rice and the place a lid on the pot, set the heat to low and let the contents cook for 47 mins then let it cool, and stir it.
2. Pour the rice in a bowl, and add to the bowl: pepper, sour cream, salt, vinegar, chili powder, lime juice, cumin, and honey.
3. Place the mix in the fridge after stirring and then fry your bacon and break it into pieces.
4. Get a bigger bowl, and combine: cilantro, rice, almonds, dressing, peas, bacon, onions, and bell peppers.
5. Place everything back in the fridge for 60 mins. Enjoy.

BACKROAD
Style Brown Rice

🥣 Prep Time: 20 mins

🕐 Total Time: 1 hr 50 mins

Servings per Recipe: 15

Calories	170 kcal
Fat	9.1 g
Carbohydrates	18.7g
Protein	4.5 g
Cholesterol	17 mg
Sodium	283 mg

Ingredients

cooking spray
1/2 C. butter
1 C. uncooked wild rice
3/4 C. uncooked brown rice
6 green onions, chopped
1 (8 oz.) package sliced mushrooms
1 (2.25 oz.) package slivered almonds
1 (10.5 oz.) can condensed French onion soup

1 (10.5 oz.) can beef consommé

Directions

1. Coat a casserole dish with nonstick spray and then set your oven to 350 degrees before doing anything else.
2. Toast your brown & wild rice in butter for 7 mins then add in the onions and cook for 4 more mins before adding the almonds, consommé, soup, and mushrooms.
3. Pour everything into your casserole dish and place a covering of foil around it. Cook the contents it in the oven for 75 mins.
4. Then stir everything.
5. Enjoy.

Easy Mexican
Style Brown Rice II

Prep Time: 20 mins
Total Time: 2 hr 20 mins

Servings per Recipe: 8

Calories	397 kcal
Fat	22.6 g
Carbohydrates	42.4g
Protein	9.1 g
Cholesterol	0 mg
Sodium	532 mg

Ingredients

2 C. cooked quinoa
1 (15 oz.) can pinto beans, rinsed and drained
1 (15 oz.) can kidney beans, rinsed and drained
1 (14 oz.) can corn
1 red onion, chopped
1 C. cooked brown rice
1 red bell pepper, chopped
1/4 C. chopped fresh cilantro

Dressing:
3/4 C. olive oil
1/3 C. red wine vinegar
1 tbsp chili powder, or to taste
2 cloves garlic, mashed
1/2 tsp salt
1/2 tsp ground black pepper
1/4 tsp cayenne pepper, or to taste

Directions

1. Get a bowl, combine: cilantro, quinoa, bell peppers, beans, rice, corn, and onions.
2. Get a 2nd bowl, combine: black and cayenne pepper, olive oil, garlic, vinegar, and chili powder.
3. Combine both bowls, then stir the mixture.
4. Place a covering over the bowl and leave it in the fridge for at least 60 mins before serving.
5. Enjoy.

CHEESY
Veggie Burgers (Vegetarian Approved)

🍲 Prep Time: 10 mins
🕐 Total Time: 20 mins

Servings per Recipe: 4	
Calories	484 kcal
Fat	9.5 g
Carbohydrates	75g
Protein	24.4 g
Cholesterol	58 mg
Sodium	1192 mg

Ingredients

1 (15 oz.) can black beans, rinsed and drained
1 C. cooked brown rice
1 small onion, finely chopped
1 egg, lightly beaten
1 C. bread crumbs
2 tbsps salsa
1/4 C. reduced-fat sour cream
1/4 C. salsa

4 hamburger buns, split
4 lettuce leaves
4 slices reduced-fat Cheddar cheese

Directions

1. Get a bowl and mash your beans in it. Then add in: salsa (2 tbsps), rice, bread crumbs, eggs, and onions.
2. Form half a C. of the mixture into patties then fry them in oil for 4 mins for each side.
3. Get a 2nd bowl, combine: salsa (4 tbsps), and sour cream.
4. Layer the following on your bun: a patty, cheddar, salsa mix, and lettuce.
5. Do this for the remaining contents.
6. Enjoy.

Cilantro
and Tea Brown Rice

🍲 Prep Time: 5 mins
🕐 Total Time: 1 hr

Servings per Recipe: 6	
Calories	150 kcal
Fat	2.9 g
Carbohydrates	27.9g
Protein	2.8 g
Cholesterol	5 mg
Sodium	20 mg

Ingredients

3 C. water
1 jasmine herbal tea bag
1 cube vegetable bouillon
1 1/2 C. uncooked brown rice
1 tbsp butter
2 tbsps chopped fresh cilantro

Directions

1. Boil your water with the tea bag as well.
2. Then take out the tea bag after 2 mins of boiling.
3. Add the bouillon and the rice.
4. Get everything boiling again, before placing a lid on the pot, setting the heat to low, and cooking the mix for 47 mins.
5. Shut the heat and once the rice has cooled off a bit stir it and add in your butter.
6. When serving add a garnishing of cilantro.
7. Enjoy.

PARSLEY, KALE
and Tofu Brown Rice

🥣 Prep Time: 20 mins

🕐 Total Time: 1 hr 35 mins

Servings per Recipe: 12

Calories	289 kcal
Fat	11.3 g
Carbohydrates	39 g
Protein	11.5 g
Cholesterol	0 mg
Sodium	770 mg

Ingredients

2 C. brown rice
4 C. water
1 (16 oz.) package extra firm tofu, diced
3/4 C. tamari almonds
1/4 C. sesame seeds
1 bunch kale, ribs removed, chopped
1/2 large head red cabbage, chopped
1 C. shredded carrot

1 C. chopped fresh flat-leaf parsley
1/2 C. chopped fresh dill
1/2 C. lemon juice
1/2 C. tamari soy sauce
2 tbsps extra-virgin olive oil
8 cloves garlic, chopped
1/4 C. stone-ground mustard
salt and ground black pepper to taste

Directions

1. Get your water and rice boiling then place a lid on the pot, set the heat to low and let the contents cook for 47 mins.
2. Add the rice to a bowl after a few mins and then put it in the fridge to get cold.
3. Meanwhile get a bowl, combine: mustard, lemon juice, olive oil, soy sauce, and garlic.
4. Take out your rice and add to the bowl: dill, tofu, parsley, almonds, carrots, sesame seeds, red cabbage, and kale.
5. Top the rice with the lemon dressing and stir everything.
6. Enjoy.

Sweet Chive
Patties

🥣 Prep Time: 15 mins
🕐 Total Time: 30 mins

Servings per Recipe: 6
Calories   285 kcal
Fat   6.1 g
Carbohydrates   53.4g
Protein   9.9 g
Cholesterol   62 mg
Sodium   620 mg

Ingredients

2 (15.25 oz.) cans whole kernel sweet corn, drained
2 C. cooked brown rice, cooled
1/2 C. skim milk
2 eggs, beaten
2 tbsps chopped fresh chives
2/3 C. whole wheat flour
2 tsps baking powder
1/8 tsp ground nutmeg

salt and ground black pepper to taste
1 tbsp olive oil, or as needed

Directions

1. Get a bowl, mix: chives, corn, eggs, rice, and milk.
2. Get a 2nd bowl, mix: black pepper, flour, salt, baking powder, and nutmeg.
3. Combine both bowls then fry a quarter of a C. of mix in olive oil for 4 mins for each side.
4. Place on paper towel to drain excess oils. Enjoy.

EASY HAWAIIAN
Style Brown Rice

🥣 Prep Time: 10 mins
🕐 Total Time: 1 hr

Servings per Recipe: 6
Calories   352 kcal
Fat   9.7 g
Carbohydrates   46.8g
Protein   21.5 g
Cholesterol   102 mg
Sodium   1033 mg

Ingredients

2 C. Minute(R) Brown Rice, uncooked
1 (20 oz.) can crushed pineapple, divided
1 (20 oz.) package ground turkey or chicken
3/4 C. green onions, thinly sliced, divided
1/2 C. teriyaki sauce, divided
1 egg, lightly beaten
1 tsp ground ginger
1/2 tsp ground nutmeg

2 tbsps orange marmalade

Directions

1. Cook the rice in line with its associated directions then set your oven to 350 degrees before doing anything else.
2. Separate half a C. of pineapple juice for later.
3. Get a bowl, combine: nutmeg, ground meat, ginger, rice, half of the teriyaki, half of the pineapple, and half of the onions.
4. Shape the mix into balls.
5. Then layer them in a casserole dish coated with nonstick spray and cook everything in the oven for 27 mins.
6. Meanwhile simmer the following remaining ingredients for 5 mins: orange marmalade, pineapple and juice, onions, and teriyaki.
7. When the meatballs are done top with the sauce.
8. Enjoy.

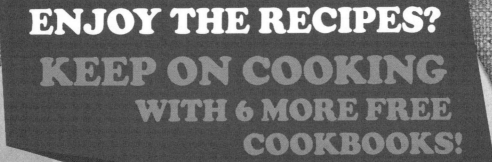

Made in the USA
Columbia, SC
02 June 2022

61173087R00033